Use of English

Ten practice tests for the
Cambridge C1 Advanced

Michael Macdonald

PROSPERITY EDUCATION

PROSPERITY EDUCATION
www.prosperityeducation.net

Registered offices: Sherlock Close, Cambridge
CB3 0HP, United Kingdom

© Prosperity Education Ltd. 2018

First published 2018

ISBN: 978-1-72-938360-5

Manufactured on demand by Kindle Direct Publishing.

This publication is in copyright. Subject to statutory exception and to the provisions of relevant collective licensing agreements, no reproduction of any part may take place without the written permission of Prosperity Education.

'Use of English', Cambridge C1 Advanced' and 'CAE' are brands belonging to The Chancellor, Masters and Scholars of the University of Cambridge and are not associated with Prosperity Education or its apps, FCE Academy and CAE Academy, and related products.

The moral rights of the author have been asserted.

For further information and resources, visit:
www.prosperityeducation.net

To infinity and beyond.

Contents

Introduction	2
About the Cambridge C1 Advanced exam	3
Prosperity Education	4
Test 1	5
Test 2	13
Test 3	21
Test 4	29
Test 5	37
Test 6	45
Test 7	53
Test 8	61
Test 9	69
Test 10	77
Answer key – Test 1	86
Answer key – Test 2	87
Answer key – Test 3	88
Answer key – Test 4	89
Answer key – Test 5	90
Answer key – Test 6	91
Answer key – Test 7	92
Answer key – Test 8	93
Answer key – Test 9	94
Answer key – Test 10	95

Introduction

Welcome to this edition of sample tests for the Cambridge C1 Advanced, Use of English (Parts 1–4).

The pass threshold of the Cambridge C1 Advanced (CAE) examination is 60% and so, in order to allow ample time for the reading parts (Parts 5–8) of Paper 1, it is advisable that candidates complete The Use of English section (Parts 1–4) as quickly as possible while maintaining accuracy. For instance, completing each part in fewer than five minutes will allow 55 minutes in which to complete the reading parts.

This resource comprises ten whole Use of English tests, answer keys, write-in answer sheets and a marking scheme, allowing you to score each test out of 36 marks.

The content has been written to closely replicate the Cambridge exam experience, and has undergone comprehensive expert and peer review. You or your students, if you are a teacher, will hopefully enjoy the wide range of essay topics and benefit from the repetitive practice, something that is key to preparing for this part of the C1 Advanced (CAE) examination.

For me, having prepared many students for this and other Cambridge exams, pre- and post-2015, when the specification changed, this is clearly the section that poses the biggest challenge. Without there being much support available by way of quality practice material, students struggle to gain the necessary levels of confidence in the Use of English section prior to sitting the exam. Therefore, in my classes, after studying and working through the core knowledge required, we drill, drill and drill exercises in preparation for the exams.

I hope that you will find this resource a useful study aid, and I wish you all the best in preparing for the exam.

Michael Macdonald
Madrid, 2018

About the C1 Advanced exam

The Use of English section of the C1 Advanced (CAE) exam is broken down into four parts:

Part 1. Multiple choice cloze	
What is being tested?	This part of the exam mostly tests vocabulary, idioms, collocations, shades of meaning, phrasal verbs, complementation, semantic precision and fixed phrases.
How does it work?	It contains a test with eight gaps, each gap prompting multiple-choice questions. Each question has four possible answers, only one of which is correct.
How is it marked?	One mark is awarded for each correct answer.

Part 2. Open cloze	
What is being tested?	This part of the exam has a lexico-grammatical focus, testing candidates' awareness and control of grammar, fixed phrasing, collocation, semantic precision and, to an extent, vocabulary (the particles/prepositions for phrasal verbs).
How does it work?	It contains a text with eight gaps, each gap representing a missing word. No hints are given: candidates must think of the correct word for each gap.
How is it marked?	One mark is awarded for each correct answer.

Part 3. Word formation	
What is being tested?	This part of the exam focuses on affixation, internal changes and compounding in word formation, and vocabulary.
How does it work?	It contains a text with eight gaps, each gap representing a missing word. Beside each gap is a 'prompt' word that must be altered in some way to complete the sentence correctly.
How is it marked?	One mark is awarded for each correct answer.

Part 4. Key word transformations	
What is being tested?	This part of the exam has a lexico-grammatical focus, testing lexis, grammar and vocabulary.
How does it work?	It contains six sentences, each followed by a 'key' word and an alternative sentence conveying the same meaning as the first but with a gap in the middle. Candidates are to use the keyword provided to complete the second sentence so that it has a similar meaning to the first sentence. Candidates cannot change the keyword provided.
How is it marked?	Each correct answer is broken down into two marks.

Prosperity Education

Prosperity Education Ltd is a Cambridge-based educational publishing company providing exam-quality test practice for the Cambridge B2 First (FCE) and C1 Advanced (CAE). All content is written, reviewed and produced by English exam preparation experts.

Visit our website www.prosperityeducation.net for free Cambridge exam resources and information on all publications.

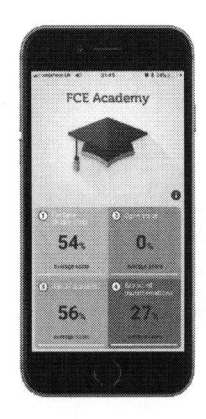

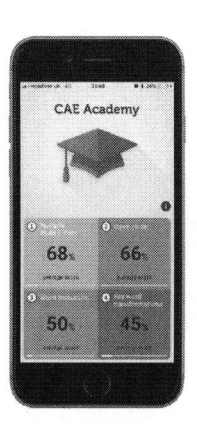

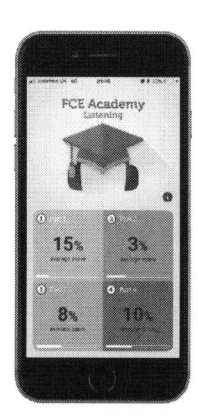

PROSPERITY EDUCATION
www.prosperityeducation.net

Cambridge C1 Advanced Use of English

Test 1

Cambridge C1 Advanced Use of English

Part 1   Multiple choice   Test 1

For questions 1–8, read the text below and decide which answer best fits each gap. In the separate answer sheet, mark the appropriate answer (A, B, C or D).

Apple Macintosh

In 1979, Apple, a successful young company in which Xerox had been (1)_____ the first to invest, was developing its Lisa computer, the second commercial machine to (2)_____ a Graphical User Interface (GUI).

Both Xerox and Apple knew that success (3)_____ in being able to precisely render an image visible on-screen onto a printed page without being (4)_____ to just one printer, (5)_____ Xerox having this very functionality in development. Apple's (6)_____ executive, the late Steve Jobs, had in the Lisa a product which he knew could change the world of office communications. However, poor sales of the computer did not (7)_____ this perspective.

(8)_____ Apple's rendition of the Graphical User Interface was a revelation in the world of green-on-black ASCII display text, it was to be the Lisa's successor, the seminal Macintosh, that would ultimately change that world.

1	A	between	B	amongst	C	one	D	partly
2	A	utilise	B	access	C	apply	D	imply
3	A	appeared	B	found	C	lay	D	became
4	A	assigned	B	detained	C	held	D	confined
5	A	however	B	despite	C	regardless	D	although
6	A	founding	B	making	C	originating	D	starting
7	A	vindicate	B	appropriate	C	indicate	D	defend
8	A	When	B	Whilst	C	Meantime	D	If

Cambridge C1 Advanced Use of English

Part 2   Open cloze   Test 1

For questions 9–16, read the text below and decide which word best fits each gap. Use only one word for each gap. In the separate answer sheet, write your answers in capital letters, using one box per letter.

Clogs

The exact origin of wooden shoes, or 'clogs', is impossible to say, although it is believed that the Germanic and Celtic cultures in Europe both enjoyed a similar type of footwear. The oldest surviving clogs date **(9)** ___in___ the 13th century and were discovered in Holland. It is of **(10)** ___very___ likely that clogs have been fabricated for thousands of years. However, **(11)** ___despite___ to the fact that they are made in part or completely from wood, older examples **(12)** ___shows___ the sturdy footwear do not exist.

Clogs **(13)** ___have been___ originally a kind of safety shoe; used in heavy labour, their rigidity gives the wearer a degree of protection from falling hazards in the workplace. Today, the shoes are found worldwide, although there are great variations in style from region to region because of **(14)** ___their___ hand-made nature.

Today, clogs remain **(15)** ___still___ beloved items of fashion wear and as part of traditional costume. They are typically purchased by tourists in countries **(16)** ___known___ as Holland, to which they have become, to some degree, synonymous.

Cambridge C1 Advanced Use of English
Part 3 — Word formation — Test 1

For questions 17–24, use the stem word on the right to form the correct word that fills each gap. In the separate answer sheet, write your answers in capital letters, using one box per letter.

Metal of mystery

It came from outer space (most of it arrived on Earth by meteorite), and you can still see it there in the visors of astronauts' helmets (it filters out (17)_____ infrared rays). **HARM**

It can be found on every continent on the planet and it is thought that 80% of it is still buried deep (18)_____. And it's not only found on land: 25 tons of it float in every (19)_____ mile of sea water. Yet, despite being found in so many places, there is hardly any of it around. (20)_____, if you compressed all of it together you would be unable to fill more than three Olympic-size swimming pools. **GROUND** **CUBE** **AMAZE**

It is a vital component of certain electronic products, such as mobile phones, GPS systems and computer hardware, and it is (21)_____ in aerospace engineering and space aviation. Back here on Earth, it has been used by dentists since 700 BC to mend broken (22)_____. Furthermore, scientists have discovered traces of it in our blood and in the dust at the side of the road. You can even eat it. **VALUE** **TOOTH**

Its name is derived from the Latin word for 'shining dawn', and when (23)_____ pure, it can be moulded by hand. **ABSOLUTE**

Which metal are we (24)_____? Gold! **DESCRIBE**

Cambridge C1 Advanced Use of English

Part 4 — Key word transformation — **Test 1**

For questions 25–30, complete the second sentence, using the word given, so that it has a similar meaning to the first sentence. Do not change the word provided and use between three and six words in total. In the separate answer sheet, write your answers in capital letters, using one box per letter.

25 If you would prefer we didn't inform you about promotions in the future, please mark the box.

RATHER

If you _____ informed of future promotions, please mark the box.

26 After the weather took a turn for the worse, the organisers had to cancel the event.

CHOICE

The weather became so bad the organisers _____ cancel the event.

27 Due to the weather the referee decided he needed to postpone the match until the following week.

OFF

It was decided the match _____ until a later date due to the weather.

28 As soon as he started singing, the crowd went crazy.

HAD

No sooner _____ than the crowd went crazy.

29 He felt much better as a result of stopping smoking.

RESULTED

Stopping smoking _____ much better.

30 I was wondering whether you would mind if she came for lunch with us.

TO

Do you have _____ lunch with us?

Answer sheet: Cambridge C1 Advanced Use of English

Test No. ☐

Mark out of 36 ☐

Name _____ **Date** _____

Part 1: Multiple choice   8 marks

Mark the appropriate answer (A, B, C or D).

| 0 | A **B** C D |

1	A B C D		5	A B C D
2	A B C D		6	A B C D
3	A B C D		7	A B C D
4	A B C D		8	A B C D

Part 2: Open cloze   8 marks

Write your answers in capital letters, using one box per letter.

| 0 | B | E | C | A | U | S | E | | | |

| 9 |
| 10 |
| 11 |
| 12 |
| 13 |
| 14 |
| 15 |
| 16 |

© 2018 Prosperity Education – Use of English, Cambridge C1 Advanced and CAE are brands belonging to The Chancellor, Masters and Scholars of the University of Cambridge and are not associated with Prosperity Education or its apps, CAE Academy and FCE Academy

Answer sheet: Cambridge C1 Advanced Use of English

Test No. ☐

Mark out of 36 ☐

Name _____ **Date** _____

Part 1: Multiple choice   8 marks

Mark the appropriate answer (A, B, C or D).

0 · A · **B** · C · D

1	A B C D		5	A B C D
2	A B C D		6	A B C D
3	A B C D		7	A B C D
4	A B C D		8	A B C D

Part 2: Open cloze   8 marks

Write your answers in capital letters, using one box per letter.

0 | B | E | C | A | U | S | E |

9 ▢
10 ▢
11 ▢
12 ▢
13 ▢
14 ▢
15 ▢
16 ▢

© 2018 Prosperity Education – Use of English, Cambridge C1 Advanced and CAE are brands belonging to The Chancellor, Masters and Scholars of the University of Cambridge and are not associated with Prosperity Education or its apps, CAE Academy and FCE Academy

Cambridge C1 Advanced Use of English

Test 2

Cambridge C1 Advanced Use of English

Part 1 — Multiple choice — Test 2

For questions 1–8, read the text below and decide which answer best fits each gap. In the separate answer sheet, mark the appropriate answer (A, B, C or D).

J.K. Rowling

Joanne Rowling was born in England in 1965 and is best **(1)**_____ to the world as the author of the 'Harry Potter' series of books. She applied to study at Oxford University, but was unsuccessful and **(2)**_____ studied at Exeter University, from where she graduated with a degree in French and Classics.

It wasn't until she was 30 years old that she completed the **(3)**_____ for *Harry Potter and the Philosopher's Stone*, having **(4)**_____ the idea for the complete series a few years earlier during a long train journey. At the time, she was living in relative poverty, dependent as a single mother on State benefits, and she completed the first book during the hours her baby, Jessica, slept.

Within a short **(5)**_____ of just five years, she would become a multi-millionaire and the UK's greatest **(6)**_____ author of all time. An **(7)**_____ businesswoman, Joanne retained the copyright to the Harry Potter franchise and holds creative control of the production of the films and the lucrative **(8)**_____ business that followed the books.

1	A	known	B	heard	C	recognised	D	familiarised
2	A	rather	B	however	C	instead	D	regardless
3	A	copy	B	manuscript	C	draft	D	core
4	A	come down with	B	come up with	C	come across as	D	come through
5	A	space	B	term	C	period	D	age
6	A	selling	B	being	C	reading	D	vending
7	A	cunning	B	astute	C	foxy	D	enlightened
8	A	enjoyment	B	recreation	C	diversion	D	entertainment

Cambridge C1 Advanced Use of English

Part 2 — Open cloze — Test 2

For questions 9–16, read the text below and decide which word best fits each gap. Use only one word for each gap. In the separate answer sheet, write your answers in capital letters, using one box per letter.

Italian football

Italy has long enjoyed an incredible reputation for the game of football, known **(9)**_____ 'calcio' from the Italian word for 'kick'. The 'blue shirts' of the Italian national team have been the recipients of the World Cup four times (second **(10)**_____ to Brazil). **(11)**_____ only that, teams from Italy have won 48 major European trophies. No wonder football is the most popular spectator sport in the country.

Italy's *Serie A*, **(12)**_____ is the top football league in the country, includes three of the world's foremost clubs. Turin's Juventus (originally a youth side, **(13)**_____ the name), was the first professional club in the country and was founded in 1897. It is the most successful club in Italy today. Two other world-renowned teams are local rivals A.C. Milan and Inter Milan. The Milanese teams share San Siro, which is the largest stadium in Italy, and their derby matches guarantee upwards **(14)**_____ 80,000 spectators.

Serie A has earned a reputation as a league for older, more experienced players, but recently Italian football has focused **(15)**_____ recruiting and training younger players **(16)**_____ a bid to compete with the UK's Premier League. It is now one of the best places to look for the future of the beautiful game.

Cambridge C1 Advanced Use of English
Part 3   Word formation   Test 2

For questions 17–24, use the stem word on the right to form the correct word that fills each gap. In the separate answer sheet, write your answers in capital letters, using one box per letter.

Vikings

Ask almost anyone to draw a Viking, and they will begin with a horned helmet and an axe. But the image of a 'fearsome' Scandinavian warrior looting the coastal **(17)**_____ of Europe is as one-sided as it is **(18)**_____. The Vikings were raiders, it is true, but also explorers, settlers, traders and mercenaries.   **SETTLE** / **ENDURE**

The **(19)**_____ Viking raids occurred in the 9th century, possibly as a response to the aggressive growth of Christian Europe to the south. Coastal **(20)**_____ were easy prey and at the time there were few vessels able to engage a Viking longship in combat.   **EARLY** / **COMMUNE**

Initially, the **(21)**_____ would return home after every conquest, but, gradually, they began to fortify and settle new lands, establishing territories in England, France, Iceland and Greenland. The Normans of northern France were a Viking community before **(22)**_____ invading England in the 11th century.   **RAID** / **SUCCESS**

There is ample evidence that Vikings reached as far as Baghdad to the East and Newfoundland to the West. Three hundred years of **(23)**_____ and trade brought about big changes in the culture of Scandinavia, and by the end of the 'Viking Age' the **(24)**_____ Christianised kingdoms of Denmark, Sweden and Norway were ready to take their place amongst the established nations of Europe.   **EXPLORE** / **NEW**

Cambridge C1 Advanced Use of English

Part 4 — Key word transformation — **Test 2**

For questions 25–30, complete the second sentence, using the word given, so that it has a similar meaning to the first sentence. Do not change the word provided and use between three and six words in total. In the separate answer sheet, write your answers in capital letters, using one box per letter.

25 I don't think you make a strong enough argument in favour of your view.

STRONGLY

You don't argue your _____ in my opinion.

26 Tim decided he had been at the party for too long and wanted to leave.

HIGH

Tim decided _____ the party.

27 Apart from being more entertaining than its competitors, the app was also more educational.

ONLY

Not _____ terms of entertainment, it was educational too.

28 The hard work you invest in your degree is compensated by the experience you get through doing it.

WORTH

The experience gained by getting a degree is what _____ for.

29 He would have got the job except that he lacked a qualification in maths.

FROM

He has all the things needed for the job _____ maths qualification.

30 Celebrities often complain about the pressure of receiving constant attention from the public.

EYE

Constantly _____ can be a cause of great stress for celebrities.

Answer sheet: Cambridge C1 Advanced
Use of English

Test No. ☐

Mark out of 36 ☐

Name _____ **Date** _____

Part 1: Multiple choice   8 marks

Mark the appropriate answer (A, B, C or D).

| 0 | A **B** C D |

1	A B C D		5	A B C D
2	A B C D		6	A B C D
3	A B C D		7	A B C D
4	A B C D		8	A B C D

Part 2: Open cloze   8 marks

Write your answers in capital letters, using one box per letter.

| 0 | B | E | C | A | U | S | E | | | |

9.
10.
11.
12.
13.
14.
15.
16.

© 2018 Prosperity Education – Use of English, Cambridge C1 Advanced and CAE are brands belonging to The Chancellor, Masters and Scholars of the University of Cambridge and are not associated with Prosperity Education or its apps, CAE Academy and FCE Academy

Part 3: Word formation

8 marks

Write your answers in capital letters, using one box per letter.

17.
18.
19.
20.
21.
22.
23.
24.

Part 4: Key word transformation

12 marks

Write your answers in capital letters, using one box per letter.

25.
26.
27.
28.
29.
30.

PROSPERITY EDUCATION
www.prosperityeducation.net

Cambridge C1 Advanced Use of English

Test 3

Cambridge C1 Advanced Use of English
Part 1   Multiple choice   Test 3

For questions 1–8, read the text below and decide which answer best fits each gap. In the separate answer sheet, mark the appropriate answer (A, B, C or D).

Polish cuisine

Poland has a long **(1)**_____ of delicious meals and visitors are sure to eat well during a visit to the country. In addition to **(2)**_____ a revival in its country of origin, Polish cuisine is also finding many new fans enthusiastically singing its **(3)**_____ in foreign countries. Breaded pork cutlets are a national dish, as are *kielbasa* sausages (which **(4)**_____ a number of varieties and colours, including white) and thin slices of beef wrapped around various stuffings. Semicircular, filled dumplings **(5)**_____ *pierogi*, may be filled with shredded cabbage, potato or meat.

In medieval **(6)**_____, spices were cheap in Poland because of trade links with Turkey and the Caucasus, which meant that sauces flavoured with nutmeg and black pepper became popular.

Polish meals are commonly served with boiled potatoes, rice, noodles or 'buckwheat'. A popularly believed **(7)**_____ is that vegetables were introduced to Polish cuisine during the reign of Sigismund I and his Italian Queen Bona at the beginning of the 16th century. According to tradition, the serving of vegetables includes shredding and serving them with lemon and sugar (and, of course, there is the ever **(8)**_____ *sauerkraut* cabbage, too).

1	A	tradition	B	script	C	story	D	theme
2	A	underpassing	B	overpassing	C	undergoing	D	overgoing
3	A	praises	B	values	C	virtues	D	songs
4	A	come with	B	come over	C	come in	D	come up with
5	A	thought of as	B	known as	C	described as	D	understood as
6	A	ages	B	times	C	years	D	eras
7	A	history	B	myth	C	account	D	description
8	A	here	B	there	C	present	D	attending

Cambridge C1 Advanced Use of English

Part 2 — Open cloze — Test 3

For questions 9–16, read the text below and decide which word best fits each gap. Use only one word for each gap. In the separate answer sheet, write your answers in capital letters, using one box per letter.

Blogging

A blog (an abbreviation of 'weblog') is an online diary **(9)**_____ which a series of posts are displayed in reverse-chronological order. Blogging emerged in the 1990s **(10)**_____ technology was created that allowed people to easily create **(11)**_____ own web pages, and the first blogs were published on platforms such as LiveJournal. Popular blog platforms in use today include Tumblr, WordPress and Google's Blogger.

Typically, bloggers write text and upload images to share **(12)**_____ their friends and family, or a wider community of followers. Most blogs have some sort of focus, whether it's books, films, gardening, music, or a particular career, and generally have small readerships. Some blogs, however, achieve greater significance. Salam Pax, the 'Baghdad Blogger', became world-famous before and during the 2003 US-led invasion of Iraq, with his account of daily life in that city.

Blogging can be a good way to further one's career, too, but **(13)**_____ are dangers. Employees have lost their jobs for their unfavourable blog descriptions of colleagues, or for inadvertently revealing confidential information.

In the news sphere, blogging has become important as traditional newspapers increasingly go **(14)**_____ of business. This increased usage has been blamed **(15)**_____ a decline in standards of reporting as many political bloggers are not trained journalists and so do not adhere **(16)**_____ professional journalistic standards.

Cambridge C1 Advanced Use of English

Part 3 — Word formation — Test 3

For questions 17–24, use the stem word on the right to form the correct word that fills each gap. In the separate answer sheet, write your answers in capital letters, using one box per letter.

Wimbledon

The Wimbledon **(17)**_____ is the world's oldest tennis tournament and is considered by many to be the most **(18)**_____. Founded in 1877, Wimbledon is one of the four 'grand slam' tournaments, the others being the French Open, the Australian Open and the US Open, and the only one to be played on grass. — **CHAMPION** / **PRESTIGE**

It takes place each July and lasts for two weeks, **(19)**_____ in the ladies' and gentlemen's 'singles' finals. The men's prize is a large trophy, which has been awarded every year since 1877, and the ladies' prize is a large silver plate. As well as the the honour of being that year's Wimbledon Champion, each winner **(20)**_____ receives more than one million pounds in prize money. — **END** / **ADD**

Even though the competition occurs in the summer time, games are often cancelled due to the **(21)**_____ of the English weather. Only one court, Central Court, has a **(22)**_____ roof to protect its players and **(23)**_____ from the British summer weather. Popular with celebrities and members of the royal family, tickets for a Wimbledon final are very **(24)**_____, as are the food and drink options available to spectators. — **PREDICT** / **RETRACT** / **SPECTATE** / **EXPENSE**

Cambridge C1 Advanced Use of English

Part 4 Key word transformation Test 3

For questions 25–30, complete the second sentence, using the word given, so that it has a similar meaning to the first sentence. Do not change the word provided and use between three and six words in total. In the separate answer sheet, write your answers in capital letters, using one box per letter.

25 I don't mind if you come today or tomorrow.

DIFFERENCE

It _____ me whether you come today or tomorrow.

26 'What are you thinking about doing for your birthday?' asked Mindy.

MIND

Mindy asked him what _____ for his birthday.

27 His team regarded the footballer so highly that they would do anything to keep him.

HELD

The player was _____ esteem by his team that they would do anything to keep him.

28 Natalie had never had a problem learning foreign languages.

COME

Learning foreign languages _____ to Natalie.

29 Someone has given you the incorrect information. The guitar is €1000, not €100.

MISINFORMED

You seem _____ as the guitar is €1000, not €100.

30 If you get there before me, which is unlikely, try to get a table.

EVENT

In _____ arriving before me, try to get a table.

Answer sheet: Cambridge C1 Advanced Use of English

Test No. ☐

Mark out of 36 ☐

Name _____ **Date** _____

Part 1: Multiple choice   8 marks

Mark the appropriate answer (A, B, C or D).

| 0 | A **B** C D |

1	A B C D		5	A B C D
2	A B C D		6	A B C D
3	A B C D		7	A B C D
4	A B C D		8	A B C D

Part 2: Open cloze   8 marks

Write your answers in capital letters, using one box per letter.

| 0 | B | E | C | A | U | S | E | | | |

9										
10										
11										
12										
13										
14										
15										
16										

© 2018 Prosperity Education – Use of English, Cambridge C1 Advanced and CAE are brands belonging to The Chancellor, Masters and Scholars of the University of Cambridge and are not associated with Prosperity Education or its apps, CAE Academy and FCE Academy

Answer sheet: Cambridge C1 Advanced Use of English

Test No. ☐

Mark out of 36 ☐

Name _____ **Date** _____

Part 1: Multiple choice — 8 marks

Mark the appropriate answer (A, B, C or D).

| 0 | A | **B** | C | D |

1	A	B	C	D		5	A	B	C	D
2	A	B	C	D		6	A	B	C	D
3	A	B	C	D		7	A	B	C	D
4	A	B	C	D		8	A	B	C	D

Part 2: Open cloze — 8 marks

Write your answers in capital letters, using one box per letter.

| 0 | B | E | C | A | U | S | E | | | |

9										
10										
11										
12										
13										
14										
15										
16										

© 2018 Prosperity Education – Use of English, Cambridge C1 Advanced and CAE are brands belonging to The Chancellor, Masters and Scholars of the University of Cambridge and are not associated with Prosperity Education or its apps, CAE Academy and FCE Academy

Cambridge C1 Advanced Use of English

Test 4

Cambridge C1 Advanced Use of English

Part 1 — Multiple choice — **Test 4**

For questions 1–8, read the text below and decide which answer best fits each gap. In the separate answer sheet, mark the appropriate answer (A, B, C or D).

App for that

The mobile phone app is a **(1)**_____ modern miracle, following its introduction with the **(2)**_____ of 'smart' mobile devices in the first decade of the 21st century.

There are now hundreds of thousands of apps available to download and their development has become big business. Companies are often technical **(3)**_____ that allow users to access the facilities of the program **(4)**_____ free of charge. Then, after seeing their **(5)**_____ reach numbers in the hundreds of millions, the app is sold to bigger companies for highly inflated sums of money (often billions of dollars).

Now, ubiquitous platforms such as WhatsApp, Facebook and Twitter **(6)**_____ their success wholly to the immense popularity of a humble app. However, apps are created for almost every purpose you can **(7)**_____, such as games, utility tools or academic training, and so the **(8)**_____ of the phrase "there's an app for that" comes as no surprise.

1	A	surely	B	probably	C	truly	D	possibly
2	A	issue	B	emergence	C	birth	D	debut
3	A	start-ups	B	beginners	C	creations	D	inaugurations
4	A	thoroughly	B	ultimately	C	fully	D	completely
5	A	audiences	B	members	C	users	D	markets
6	A	owe	B	debt	C	blame	D	define
7	A	think	B	imagine	C	dream	D	conjure
8	A	making	B	inventing	C	coming	D	coining

Cambridge C1 Advanced Use of English

Part 2 Open cloze Test 4

For questions 9–16, read the text below and decide which word best fits each gap. Use only one word for each gap. In the separate answer sheet, write your answers in capital letters, using one box per letter.

Freerunning

Freerunning, also known **(9)**_____ *Parkour*, is the art of running through the urban environment. Its participants can be seen leaping from roof to roof, scaling high walls, and balancing over perilous drops.

Georges Hébert first developed the system of military obstacle course training called *Parcour*, or *Parkour*, before France's war in Indochina. Soldiers **(10)**_____ trained to move quickly and athletically through obstacles. In France in the 1990s, a small group of enthusiasts named the *Yamakasi*, inspired **(11)**_____ *Parkour* and the martial arts movies of Jackie Chan, developed these ideas **(12)**_____ an impressive but inherently dangerous hobby.

Prominent freerunner Sébastien Foucan describes the concepts of the discipline in his 2003 book *Freerunning: Find your way*. He claims the central idea behind freerunning is **(13)**_____ a human being should move fluidly through his or her environment.

Freerunning **(14)**_____ came to the attention of the wider world through the 2003 documentary *Jump London* and has been growing in popularity ever **(15)**_____. Representatives of the sport **(16)**_____ currently in discussions with the International Olympic Committee (IOC) to see if it can be legitimised as an official Olympic sport.

Cambridge C1 Advanced Use of English
Part 3   Word formation   Test 4

For questions 17–24, use the stem word on the right to form the correct word that fills each gap. In the separate answer sheet, write your answers in capital letters, using one box per letter.

Crowdfunding

Crowdfunding is a **(17)**_____ way to raise money for your **(18)**_____, project, or crazy idea and there exist many success stories. To build their groundbreaking virtual reality headset, for instance, Oculus Rift raised $2.4 million dollars through crowdfunding alone. However, the **(19)**_____ of projects fail to get the funding they need, and therefore fail to get off the ground.   **FANTASY**   **INVENT**   **MAJOR**

Here are three top tips to crowdfunding success:

1. Talk the talk

People won't want to invest in something that comes across as amateurish or ill-thought-out. You have to make your idea look great! Invest time in **(20)**_____ your proposition, think **(21)**_____ about how to make your video sell your idea, and, most **(22)**_____, make sure that your text is accurate.   **PERFECT**   **CARE**   **IMPORT**

2. Develop your audience before you pitch your idea

(23)_____ a new comic book? Get onto the comic book fan websites and make friends. Invented a great new game? Write a blog about it. A new kind of paintbrush? Start a YouTube art channel. Then, when you are ready to begin your campaign, your early adopters are ready to be approached.   **PUBLISH**

3. Keep talking

Don't just launch your idea and sit back. Take a fortnight off work and spend every day **(24)**_____ people about your business campaign.   **TELL**

Cambridge C1 Advanced Use of English

Part 4 — Key word transformation — **Test 4**

For questions 25–30, complete the second sentence, using the word given, so that it has a similar meaning to the first sentence. Do not change the word provided and use between three and six words in total. In the separate answer sheet, write your answers in capital letters, using one box per letter.

25 All the teacher's hard work didn't make any difference as the students didn't study.

CONSEQUENCE

All the teacher's hard work _____ because the students didn't study.

26 The value of the currency gradually rose as the country's prosperity continued.

GRADUAL

A _____ currency accompanied the country's continued prosperity.

27 The company decided to reappraise its strategy thoroughly.

THOROUGH

It was decided that there needed to _____ the company's strategy.

28 He got fired because he arrived late for work.

TIME

If only _____ he wouldn't have been fired.

29 At the start of the year the government introduced a ban on smoking in public places.

ILLEGAL

The government made _____ in public places at the start of the year.

30 'Please do not allow your children to feed the animals', announced the sign at the entrance of the zoo.

LET

The zoo advised visitors _____ feed the animals.

Answer sheet: Cambridge C1 Advanced Use of English

Test No. ☐

Mark out of 36 ☐

Name _____ **Date** _____

Part 1: Multiple choice   8 marks

Mark the appropriate answer (A, B, C or D).

| 0 | A **B** C D |

1	A B C D		5	A B C D
2	A B C D		6	A B C D
3	A B C D		7	A B C D
4	A B C D		8	A B C D

Part 2: Open cloze   8 marks

Write your answers in capital letters, using one box per letter.

| 0 | B | E | C | A | U | S | E | | | |

| 9 |
| 10 |
| 11 |
| 12 |
| 13 |
| 14 |
| 15 |
| 16 |

© 2018 Prosperity Education – Use of English, Cambridge C1 Advanced and CAE are brands belonging to The Chancellor, Masters and Scholars of the University of Cambridge and are not associated with Prosperity Education or its apps, CAE Academy and FCE Academy

Answer sheet: Cambridge C1 Advanced Use of English

Test No. ☐

Mark out of 36 ☐

Name _____ **Date** _____

Part 1: Multiple choice   8 marks

Mark the appropriate answer (A, B, C or D).

0 A **B** C D

1	A B C D		5	A B C D
2	A B C D		6	A B C D
3	A B C D		7	A B C D
4	A B C D		8	A B C D

Part 2: Open cloze   8 marks

Write your answers in capital letters, using one box per letter.

0 | B | E | C | A | U | S | E |

9
10
11
12
13
14
15
16

© 2018 Prosperity Education – Use of English, Cambridge C1 Advanced and CAE are brands belonging to The Chancellor, Masters and Scholars of the University of Cambridge and are not associated with Prosperity Education or its apps, CAE Academy and FCE Academy

PROSPERITY EDUCATION
www.prosperityeducation.net

Cambridge C1 Advanced Use of English

Test 5

Cambridge C1 Advanced Use of English

Part 1 Multiple choice Test 5

For questions 1–8, read the text below and decide which answer best fits each gap. In the separate answer sheet, mark the appropriate answer (A, B, C or D).

Stephen Hawking

Stephen Hawking was a **(1)**_____ cosmologist and theoretical physicist and the Director for Research at the University of Cambridge Centre for Theoretical Cosmology. He was also a **(2)**_____ author, whose book *A Brief History of Time*, in which his theories of relativity and black holes are presented in **(3)**_____ terms, sold millions of copies.

Born in 1942 in Oxford, England, Hawking was privately educated before **(4)**_____ admission to Oxford University, where he studied physics and was part of a college rowing team. As an **(5)**_____ student, he received a first-class undergraduate degree and decided to **(6)**_____ his academic studies at Cambridge University, where he obtained his PhD in Applied Mathematics and Theoretical Physics, specialising in general relativity and cosmology.

From an early age, Stephen **(7)**_____ from Motor Neurone Disease, from which he gradually became paralysed and **(8)**_____ to a mechanical wheelchair. The disease also removed his ability to speak for himself and so he relied on special speech software to project a voice for the words he typed. He died in 2018, mourned by millions.

1	A	world-acclaimed	B	world-honoured	C	world-famous	D	world-noted
2	A	best-selling	B	high-selling	C	up-selling	D	sell-out
3	A	lego	B	layperson	C	novice	D	simpleton
4	A	improving	B	gaining	C	winning	D	getting
5	A	important	B	underlined	C	emboldened	D	outstanding
6	A	chase	B	pursue	C	seek	D	go
7	A	suffered	B	pained	C	hurt	D	sickened
8	A	stuck	B	restrained	C	confined	D	depended

© 2018 Prosperity Education – Use of English, Cambridge C1 Advanced and CAE are brands belonging to The Chancellor, Masters and Scholars of the University of Cambridge and are not associated with Prosperity Education or its apps, CAE Academy and FCE Academy

Cambridge C1 Advanced Use of English

Part 2 — Open cloze — **Test 5**

For questions 9–16, read the text below and decide which word best fits each gap. Use only one word for each gap. In the separate answer sheet, write your answers in capital letters, using one box per letter.

Breakfast

Breakfast is the most important meal of the day, or so they say, and its content varies greatly from region to region. Named **(9)**_____ its country of origin, the Full English Breakfast is a hearty feast which usually consists **(10)**_____ meat, eggs, bread and beans. Good for the soul, but not for your health!

In fact, it seems a link can be drawn **(11)**_____ the types of breakfast eaten in each part of the world and the local climate. In Mediterranean countries, for instance, lighter ingredients, such as olives and tomatoes, are usually accompanied **(12)**_____ bread. Spanish children, meanwhile, find biscuits and chocolate drink an acceptable way to start the day.

Breakfast cereals from well-known producers are **(13)**_____ business, with each brand potentially generating huge incomes. Due to this, these companies have made great efforts to instil a breakfast cereal culture in countries **(14)**_____ one has never existed before, such as in southern Europe and the Far East.

The most important meal of the day has **(15)**_____ been so attractive, thanks **(16)**_____ well-constructed advertising campaigns.

Cambridge C1 Advanced Use of English

Part 3 — Word formation — Test 5

For questions 17–24, use the stem word on the right to form the correct word that fills each gap. In the separate answer sheet, write your answers in capital letters, using one box per letter.

Whitby

Whitby is a seaside town on the north-eastern coast of England, which **(17)**_____ has a charm and character not found in many places. Standing in the harbour are relics of the past that help illustrate its **(18)**_____ history. **DOUBT**

REMARK

On the West Cliff stands the arched upper jawbone of a whale, reflective of Whitby's strong fishing tradition and the still evident community of **(19)**_____. On the East Cliff, you can climb 199 steps to visit the ghostly ruins of Whitby Abbey and the **(20)**_____ St Mary's church and graveyard, which stand side by side, silhouetted against the dramatic clifftops and stunning Yorkshire moors. Indeed, it is here that Bram Stoker's **(21)**_____ vampire Dracula is said to have first landed on English soil. This is commemorated by a tourist attraction which includes exhibits that **(22)**_____ his story and legend. **FISH**

MAGNIFICENCE

FAME

COUNT

No visit to Whitby would be complete without having fish and chips, making it a place **(23)**_____ worth visiting. Newer **(24)**_____ to the town, loved by tourists and locals alike, are an eclectic mix of vintage shops and cafés. **DEFINE**

ADD

Cambridge C1 Advanced Use of English

Part 4 — Key word transformation — **Test 5**

For questions 25–30, complete the second sentence, using the word given, so that it has a similar meaning to the first sentence. Do not change the word provided and use between three and six words in total. In the separate answer sheet, write your answers in capital letters, using one box per letter.

25 Tony's problems with the police came as a surprise to his boss.

UNAWARE

Tony's boss _____ with the police.

26 Stephanie didn't feel like going to the gym today.

MOOD

Stephanie wasn't _____ the gym today.

27 The managers did not give recognition to how important staff morale was.

FAILED

The management _____ of staff morale.

28 The doctor enquired as to whether her health had improved.

ANY

'Was there _____ last month?' asked the doctor.

29 We'll send the books on receipt of your payment.

SOON

We'll send your books _____ your payment.

30 Because the hotel has increased the price of its rooms, I won't be coming back this year.

UP

If the hotel _____ the cost of its rooms, I would have come back this year.

Answer sheet: Cambridge C1 Advanced Use of English

Test No. ☐

Mark out of 36 ☐

Name _____   Date _____

Part 1: Multiple choice — 8 marks

Mark the appropriate answer (A, B, C or D).

| 0 | A **B** C D |

1	A B C D		5	A B C D
2	A B C D		6	A B C D
3	A B C D		7	A B C D
4	A B C D		8	A B C D

Part 2: Open cloze — 8 marks

Write your answers in capital letters, using one box per letter.

| 0 | B | E | C | A | U | S | E | | | |

9. ☐☐☐☐☐☐☐☐☐☐
10. ☐☐☐☐☐☐☐☐☐☐
11. ☐☐☐☐☐☐☐☐☐☐
12. ☐☐☐☐☐☐☐☐☐☐
13. ☐☐☐☐☐☐☐☐☐☐
14. ☐☐☐☐☐☐☐☐☐☐
15. ☐☐☐☐☐☐☐☐☐☐
16. ☐☐☐☐☐☐☐☐☐☐

© 2018 Prosperity Education – Use of English, Cambridge C1 Advanced and CAE are brands belonging to The Chancellor, Masters and Scholars of the University of Cambridge and are not associated with Prosperity Education or its apps, CAE Academy and FCE Academy

Answer sheet: Cambridge C1 Advanced
Use of English

Test No. [ ]

Mark out of 36 [ ]

Name _____   **Date** _____

Part 1: Multiple choice   8 marks

Mark the appropriate answer (A, B, C or D).

| 0 | A | **B** | C | D |

1	A B C D		5	A B C D
2	A B C D		6	A B C D
3	A B C D		7	A B C D
4	A B C D		8	A B C D

Part 2: Open cloze   8 marks

Write your answers in capital letters, using one box per letter.

| 0 | B | E | C | A | U | S | E |

9.
10.
11.
12.
13.
14.
15.
16.

# Cambridge C1 Advanced Use of English

Test 6

Cambridge C1 Advanced Use of English

Part 1 Multiple choice Test 6

For questions 1–8, read the text below and decide which answer best fits each gap. In the separate answer sheet, mark the appropriate answer (A, B, C or D).

Facebook

The social media application was **(1)**_____ in 2004 and launched on the 4th of February that year by five students from Harvard University. The website was **(2)**_____ intended for Harvard students, **(3)**_____ it quickly became used in other academic institutions and, since 2006, Facebook has been available to the **(4)**_____ public. By the end of 2016 Facebook had about 1.8 billion active monthly users.

The app can be accessed from any web-connected device, with the growth of the mobile phone adding to its **(5)**_____ popularity. Users connect with each other, sending 'friend **(6)**_____' to people they know, or would like to get to know.

Participants 'post' status updates and their own photos, and can 'check in' to a location, sharing their whereabouts with their friends and followers. Facebook has come in for some **(7)**_____ criticism from certain quarters because of the amount of information it collects on its users, including their likes and dislikes, which have valuable marketing revenue potential. However, the company **(8)**_____ that all the information collected by the company is freely provided by its users.

1	A	set up	B	brought up	C	raised up	D	ended up
2	A	essentially	B	principally	C	initially	D	singularly
3	A	therefore	B	however	C	albeit	D	hence
4	A	mass	B	normal	C	whole	D	general
5	A	phenomenal	B	giant	C	great	D	big
6	A	requirements	B	solicitations	C	requests	D	permissions
7	A	stiff	B	hard	C	rigid	D	solid
8	A	points to	B	singles out	C	points out	D	counts on

Cambridge C1 Advanced Use of English
Part 2　　　　　　　　　　Open cloze　　　　　　　　　　Test 6

For questions 9–16, read the text below and decide which word best fits each gap. Use only one word for each gap. In the separate answer sheet, write your answers in capital letters, using one box per letter.

Carnival

The annual Brazilian Carnival is traditionally a religious festival that takes place at the beginning of Lent, the 40-day period before Easter. The word 'carnival', comes **(9)**_____ the Latin *carnevelare*, and literally means 'to remove meat', which is what many Roman Catholics do to their diet **(10)**_____ Lent.

In Rio de Janeiro and elsewhere across the country, you can be a spectator to a large parade of people dressed **(11)**_____ colourful costume and dancing through the streets to samba music. It is the world's biggest carnival, **(12)**_____ attendances of more **(13)**_____ two million people each day. It comprises individual processions by numerous samba schools, which are collaborations of neighbours who wish to take part. The most famous dance is called 'carnival samba', **(14)**_____ is a Brazilian dance of African origin. The *batacuda*-style music is percussion-based and provides the rhythm to which the dancers and spectators move.

More than 300 musical groups, or *bandas*, take **(15)**_____ in each parade, making this the most popular street party **(16)**_____ the world.

Cambridge C1 Advanced Use of English

Part 3   Word formation   Test 6

For questions 17–24, use the stem word on the right to form the correct word that fills each gap. In the separate answer sheet, write your answers in capital letters, using one box per letter.

The Mary Rose

The *Mary Rose* was one of the most important ships in the fleet of King Henry VIII of England (who reigned between 1509 and 1547). For her time, she would have been an enormous and, no doubt, **(17)**_____ craft, capable of carrying 200 sailors, 185 soldiers and 30 gunners.   **IMPRESS**

She has also been of great **(18)**_____ in the field of maritime archaeology, as, in 1982, she was raised from the seabed in a **(19)**_____ ambitious salvage project.   **SIGNIFY** / **HUGE**

Research divers found weaponry, tools, **(20)**_____ supplies, personal effects, and of course the bodies of many of the officers and crew (as well as a dog **(21)**_____ to have been employed to catch rats). The remains of the ship can now be seen at the Portsmouth Historic Dockyard in south-west England.   **NAVY** / **THINK**

The *Mary Rose* was first launched in 1511 and was involved in naval campaigns until 1545, when she was **(22)**_____ in a battle against a French invasion fleet. It is still unclear why she sank. One **(23)**_____ is that she had simply become too heavy following a refit, but **(24)**_____ now think human error was to blame.   **SINK** / **EXPLAIN** / **HISTORY**

Whatever the reason, Henry's loss was history's gain.

Cambridge C1 Advanced Use of English

Part 4 — Key word transformation — **Test 6**

For questions 25–30, complete the second sentence, using the word given, so that it has a similar meaning to the first sentence. Do not change the word provided and use between three and six words in total. In the separate answer sheet, write your answers in capital letters, using one box per letter.

25 They had to interrupt because of a problem in the main office.

CAUSED

The _____ a problem in the main office.

26 It's thanks to Sarah's great ideas that we found such a perfect present.

FOR

If _____ Sarah's great ideas, we wouldn't have found such a perfect present.

27 Peter was the only one in the office who didn't come to the party.

EXCEPTION

Everyone in the office _____ to the party.

28 The plane was supposed to have taken off three hours ago.

DUE

The plane _____ three hours ago.

29 He said sorry for not being able to complete the work on time.

COULD

He said he was _____ complete the work on time.

30 Even though we try really hard, my sister and I can´t get on.

MATTER

My sister and I don't have a good relationship _____ we try.

Answer sheet: Cambridge C1 Advanced Use of English

Test No. [ ]

Mark out of 36 [ ]

Name _____   **Date** _____

Part 1: Multiple choice   8 marks

Mark the appropriate answer (A, B, C or D).

0 A **B** C D

1 A B C D   5 A B C D
2 A B C D   6 A B C D
3 A B C D   7 A B C D
4 A B C D   8 A B C D

Part 2: Open cloze   8 marks

Write your answers in capital letters, using one box per letter.

0 | B | E | C | A | U | S | E |

9
10
11
12
13
14
15
16

© 2018 Prosperity Education – Use of English, Cambridge C1 Advanced and CAE are brands belonging to The Chancellor, Masters and Scholars of the University of Cambridge and are not associated with Prosperity Education or its apps, CAE Academy and FCE Academy

Part 3: Word formation 8 marks

Write your answers in capital letters, using one box per letter.

17.
18.
19.
20.
21.
22.
23.
24.

Part 4: Key word transformation 12 marks

Write your answers in capital letters, using one box per letter.

25.

26.

27.

28.

29.

30.

Cambridge C1 Advanced Use of English

Test 7

Cambridge C1 Advanced Use of English

Part 1 — Multiple choice — **Test 7**

For questions 1–8, read the text below and decide which answer best fits each gap. In the separate answer sheet, mark the appropriate answer (A, B, C or D).

Book production

The desktop publishing revolution of the 1980s continues to power and inspire the publishing **(1)**_____: what began as desktop publishing in 1984 has evolved into what is now commonly **(2)**_____ to, across all forms of modern publishing, as the Digital Revolution.

This revolution **(3)**_____ improvements to the time and cost with which books were produced and in just five years the industry had irreversibly changed, and with it the way books were produced. However, it can be said that this great **(4)**_____ came at a price: the general quality standard of printed **(5)**_____ was changed accordingly. Book production at Cambridge University Press, the world's oldest publisher, has evolved with the industry, adapting at its **(6)**_____ to successive technological **(7)**_____ throughout a four-hundred-year manufacturing legacy.

From Johannes Gutenburg's printing press of 1450 to the introduction of phototypesetting in the 1970s, Cambridge University Press has **(8)**_____ to remain the vanguard of innovation and content production, anticipating as best it can the near and distant futures of print and electronic publication.

1	A	industry	B	institution	C	factory	D	commerce
2	A	called	B	referred	C	signalled	D	cited
3	A	began	B	converted	C	affected	D	brought
4	A	invention	B	innovation	C	creation	D	introduction
5	A	output	B	crop	C	yield	D	turnout
6	A	foremost	B	limelight	C	forefront	D	spearhead
7	A	changes	B	diverts	C	alterations	D	transits
8	A	driven	B	strived	C	lead	D	promised

Cambridge C1 Advanced Use of English

Part 2 — Open cloze — Test 7

For questions 9–16, read the text below and decide which word best fits each gap. Use only one word for each gap. In the separate answer sheet, write your answers in capital letters, using one box per letter.

The Mandela Effect

'Confabulation' is the term used to describe an unconscious change in someone's memory concerning the details of a particular event, **(9)**_____ results in them remembering that event differently to how it actually happened. When groups of individuals experience the same confabulation of memory, **(10)**_____ phenomenon is attributed to the 'parallel universe theory', **(11)**_____ which, it is suggested, a possibly infinite number of universes exist, with each one producing minutely different realities to the other.

This collective confabulation of memory is **(12)**_____ as the 'Mandela Effect', so called because of the apparent collective memory held **(13)**_____ a large group of people that Nelson Mandela, the revolutionary, freedom fighter and late president of South Africa, died in 1990 while incarcerated on Robben Island. This is **(14)**_____ the historical fact that he was released from prison in 1990 and passed away many years later, in 2013.

The 'Mandela Effect' is also attributed **(15)**_____ differences in collective memory of certain popular films, **(16)**_____ notably the Tom Hanks film *Forrest Gump*, in which, for many, the line, 'My mother said life is a box of chocolates, you never know what you're going to get,' appears to have changed to: 'My mother said life *was* like a box of chocolates...'.

Cambridge C1 Advanced Use of English
Part 3   Word formation   Test 7

For questions 17–24, use the stem word on the right to form the correct word that fills each gap. In the separate answer sheet, write your answers in capital letters, using one box per letter.

The Giants' Causeway

The world-**(17)**_____ Giants' Causeway is located on the coast of County Antrim, in **(18)**_____ Ireland, and is considered to be one of the **(19)**_____ natural wonders of the United Kingdom. It is made up of thousands of interlocking basalt columns, which are the result of an ancient **(20)**_____ eruption that occurred some 50 million years ago.

FAME

NORTH

GREAT

VOLCANO

These **(21)**_____ columns lead from the land out into the Irish Sea, where they **(22)**_____, and there are identical columns on the **(23)**_____ side of the sea giving the impression that the structure is in fact a land bridge, or causeway, between Ireland and Scotland which, according to legend, was created when Irish giant Finn MacCool was challenged to a fight by the **(24)**_____ giant, Benandonner.

HEXAGON

APPEAR

NEIGHBOUR

SCOTLAND

In 1986, the Giant's Causeway was declared a UNESCO World Heritage Site and, since then, has attracted many visitors from around the world.

Cambridge C1 Advanced Use of English

Part 4 — Key word transformation — **Test 7**

For questions 25–30, complete the second sentence, using the word given, so that it has a similar meaning to the first sentence. Do not change the word provided and use between three and six words in total. In the separate answer sheet, write your answers in capital letters, using one box per letter.

25 Marta gave the impression that she was unhappy at the meeting.
    ACROSS
    Marta _____ unhappy at the meeting.

26 She didn't mention us meeting several years before.
    REFERENCE
    She _____ us meeting several years before.

27 There is no connection between the problem last year and the current problem.
    NOTHING
    This problem _____ what happened last year.

28 There has been a sharp rise in the price of electricity this year.
    RISEN
    The price of electricity _____ this year.

29 I had waited for an hour and I was just about to leave when she turned up.
    POINT
    Having waited for an hour, I was _____ when she finally arrived.

30 We had fewer problems on the excursion than we did last year.
    SO
    The excursion this year was _____ as the previous one had been.

Part 3: Word formation   8 marks

Write your answers in capital letters, using one box per letter.

17.
18.
19.
20.
21.
22.
23.
24.

Part 4: Key word transformation   12 marks

Write your answers in capital letters, using one box per letter.

25.
26.
27.
28.
29.
30.

Part 3: Word formation 8 marks

Write your answers in capital letters, using one box per letter.

17.
18.
19.
20.
21.
22.
23.
24.

Part 4: Key word transformation 12 marks

Write your answers in capital letters, using one box per letter.

25.
26.
27.
28.
29.
30.

Cambridge
C1 Advanced
Use of English

Test 8

Cambridge C1 Advanced Use of English

Part 1 — Multiple choice — Test 8

For questions 1–8, read the text below and decide which answer best fits each gap. In the separate answer sheet, mark the appropriate answer (A, B, C or D).

Robin Hood

Robin Hood was a popular hero who 'stole from the rich to give to the poor', **(1)**_____ to English folklore and tradition. **(2)**_____ or not there really was a person named Robin Hood who lived the outlaw life in the forest with a 'merry band of men' is unknown.

Some historians believe that 'Robin Hood' was in fact an alias used by thieves of the time and that the legend arose because there were so many **(3)**_____ of activities attributed to the name. Certainly there are stories from many different English regions **(4)**_____ with Robin. For instance, he may also have been a figurehead for opposition to the Norman rulers of England. The stories of Robin Hood often involve other **(5)**_____ characters, such as the forest-dwelling giant Little John, the greedy monk Friar Tuck, Will Scarlet and Robin's love interest, Maid Marian. The villain of the story is the Sheriff of Nottingham, who is **(6)**_____ as a money-grabbing tyrant with a hatred of Robin Hood.

Poems, songs and plays about Robin Hood can be **(7)**_____ back to the 12th century, and the story has been **(8)**_____ for TV and Hollywood many times.

1	A	agreeing	B	according	C	associated	D	given
2	A	Therefore	B	Even	C	Whether	D	Since
3	A	accounts	B	versions	C	histories	D	recounts
4	A	joined	B	combined	C	grouped	D	associated
5	A	memorable	B	remembered	C	indelible	D	reminded
6	A	portrayed	B	placed	C	produced	D	played
7	A	traced	B	followed	C	found	D	copied
8	A	applied	B	changed	C	adapted	D	altered

Cambridge C1 Advanced Use of English

Part 2　　　　　　　　　　Open cloze　　　　　　　　　　Test 8

For questions 9–16, read the text below and decide which word best fits each gap. Use only one word for each gap. In the separate answer sheet, write your answers in capital letters, using one box per letter.

Off the grid

Living 'off-grid' essentially means living without access to public utilities and services, **(9)**_____ as electricity, gas and water. Some people decide to drastically change their way of living, **(10)**_____ for financial or ethical reasons, or both, and in return cut down on their carbon footprint and financial outgoings.

Already popular as a way of life in Africa, it is something that more and more people in the western world make the change **(11)**_____ each year. It is estimated that 1.7 billion people now live independently 'off the grid'. Increasingly, governments encourage their citizens to instal certain equipment, such as solar and wind power generators, in **(12)**_____ homes in order that the environmental impact of global over-population may be reduced.

Eventually, **(13)**_____ generating your own energy, and by doing so **(14)**_____ a well-designed, thermally insulated building, you could be **(15)**_____ to sell excess energy to the national energy grid. So, you could be living *off* the grid and selling *to* the grid at **(16)**_____ same time.

Cambridge C1 Advanced Use of English
Part 3   Word formation   Test 8

For questions 17–24, use the stem word on the right to form the correct word that fills each gap. In the separate answer sheet, write your answers in capital letters, using one box per letter.

Ryanair

Ryanair is an Irish airline that achieved (17)_____ success following the (18)_____ of the European aviation industry in 1997, when smaller airlines could finally compete with the large operators. Co-founded in 1984 by Tony Ryan, a prominent Irish (19)_____, the company grew quickly from owning a single 15-seat light aircraft, which flew between Ireland and England, to more than 360 Boeing 737 aircraft.

COMMERCE
REGULATE

BUSINESS

(20)_____, it is the largest European airline, employing more than 1,200 pilots, and serves 32 countries in Europe, Africa and the Middle East. Chief Executive Michael O'Leary knew from the start that the key to dominating the commercial European air-travel market was to operate a single type of aircraft for a single, standard class of passenger and to reduce turnaround times at airports, (21)_____ the number of journeys each aircraft could make. By doing this, Ryanair was able to offer (22)_____ cheap fares at a time when air travel was expensive.

CURRENT

MAXIMUM

COMPARE

A series of (23)_____ airlines followed in Ryanair's footsteps, all of which adhered to the same simplified operating principles. However, Ryanair has retained its market (24)_____, largely due to its decision to improve the Ryanair customer experience in 2013.

COMPETE

DOMINATE

Cambridge C1 Advanced Use of English

Part 4 — Key word transformation — **Test 8**

For questions 25–30, complete the second sentence, using the word given, so that it has a similar meaning to the first sentence. Do not change the word provided and use between three and six words in total. In the separate answer sheet, write your answers in capital letters, using one box per letter.

25 The event had to be cancelled because of a big storm.

RESULTED

A big storm _____ of the event.

26 Alex is an expert when it comes to music.

CONCERNED

As _____, Alex is an expert.

27 Sebastian's mum thought he really should be more responsible and get a job.

HIGH

'It's _____ a job and started being more responsible', said Sebastian's mum.

28 'Is there any possibility of us getting the contract?'

CHANCE

'Do you think we are _____ winning the contract?'

29 Mr Jones greatly impressed the new students with his interesting classes and humorous stories.

MADE

Mr Jones' interesting classes and humorous stories _____ on the new students.

30 If the project is not perfectly prepared we may lose the contract.

COST

A lack of perfect _____ the contract.

Part 3: Word formation   8 marks

Write your answers in capital letters, using one box per letter.

17.
18.
19.
20.
21.
22.
23.
24.

Part 4: Key word transformation   12 marks

Write your answers in capital letters, using one box per letter.

25.
26.
27.
28.
29.
30.

Part 3: Word formation

8 marks

Write your answers in capital letters, using one box per letter.

17.
18.
19.
20.
21.
22.
23.
24.

Part 4: Key word transformation

12 marks

Write your answers in capital letters, using one box per letter.

25.
26.
27.
28.
29.
30.

Cambridge C1 Advanced Use of English

Test 9

Cambridge C1 Advanced Use of English

Part 1 — Multiple choice — Test 9

For questions 1–8, read the text below and decide which answer best fits each gap. In the separate answer sheet, mark the appropriate answer (A, B, C or D).

Top Gear

The BBC's **(1)**_____ motoring programme first aired in 2002. It has become the most **(2)**_____ factual television programme in the world. According to the *Daily Telegraph* newspaper, *Top Gear* was sold to 214 'territories', gaining a total global viewership **(3)**_____ to be 350 million.

It is in **(4)**_____ a motor-vehicle review show, and originally served to advise potential buyers of the pros and cons, such as reliability and cost, of buying a particular car. Where *Top Gear* began and continues to differ from any previous programme of its type is in its inclusion of weird and **(5)**_____ vehicles that interest the typical man or woman (but which they would probably never drive).

It also contains interviews with celebrities, **(6)**_____ humour, and races and challenges for the presenters and guests. From time to time, the alternative, wacky style **(7)**_____ more on the presenters' adventures than on the motor vehicles themselves. That, mixed with the high-octane fun of driving and testing some of the world's best and most expensive sports cars, has **(8)**_____ the show's success to date.

1	A	flagship	B	bellwether	C	forerunning	D	leading
2	A	widely observed	B	widely watched	C	heartily watched	D	deeply observed
3	A	estimated	B	guessed	C	approximated	D	counted
4	A	nature	B	root	C	essence	D	core
5	A	wonderful	B	amazing	C	fabulous	D	tremendous
6	A	onto-the-mark	B	close-to-the-bone	C	close-to-the-limit	D	over-the-line
7	A	focuses	B	fixes	C	delivers	D	keeps
8	A	guaranteed	B	sponsored	C	sealed	D	ranted

Cambridge C1 Advanced Use of English

Part 2 — Open cloze — **Test 9**

For questions 9–16, read the text below and decide which word best fits each gap. Use only one word for each gap. In the separate answer sheet, write your answers in capital letters, using one box per letter.

The Great Outdoors

I remember my earliest experience of the great outdoors: a weekend camping trip **(9)**_____ my fellow cub scouts. It must have been on the West coast. My parents always took us on holidays to seaside hotels, which were fun but very regimented and, frankly **(10)**_____, quite monotonous.

That scout camp was my first experience of sleeping in a tent, staying up long into the evening with a campfire and a pan **(11)**_____ of sausages for supper, and waking at dawn to the sound of birdsong. During this trip I **(12)**_____ a taste for the great outdoors, something which I have never forgotten or lost.

As a youngster I became an amateur naturalist, wandering ever further **(13)**_____ the local countryside to look for signs of wildlife. I can remember my delight when I discovered my first fox hole in a wooded area next to a field a few miles from my home. I soon became a keen birdwatcher and **(14)**_____ a local club that organised trips to sites of interest across the UK.

My **(15)**_____ children have been camping many times, and we treasure photos of them watching their first sunset from the doorway of our tent, but I often wonder if they will hanker **(16)**_____ hotel holidays by the seaside instead.

Cambridge C1 Advanced Use of English

Part 3 — Word formation — Test 9

For questions 17–24, use the stem word on the right to form the correct word that fills each gap. In the separate answer sheet, write your answers in capital letters, using one box per letter.

Fastest Man Alive

Usain Bolt is a Jamaican sprinter, and was born in 1986. With his two siblings, he was brought up by his parents, who ran a greengrocers in his hometown, where he played football and cricket as a (17)_____. However, after realising how quickly he could run, Bolt turned his (18)_____ to running. **YOUNG** **ATTENTIVE**

He won his first medal for coming 2nd in a school sports day and, later, at the age of just 17, in the 2002 World Junior (19)_____, he won the 200-metre race. **CHAMPION**

Bolt's first landmark (20)_____ came in the 2008 Beijing Olympics where he won three gold medals for the 100- and 200-metre sprints, and the 4x100-metre relays. He repeated the feat in 2012, and, (21)_____, once again in 2016. This final Olympic win was marred, however, when the Jamaican relay team was stripped of that 9th gold due to a team-mate's (22)_____ to pass a drugs test. Bolt has always been a strong advocate for such tests and has been a role model for his (23)_____. **ACHIEVE** **INCREDIBLE** **FAIL** **GENERATE**

He considers himself, albeit jokingly, to sit amongst the ranks of Michael Jordan and Muhammad Ali, legends in their (24)_____ sports. **RESPECT**

Cambridge C1 Advanced Use of English

Part 4 Key word transformation Test 9

For questions 25–30, complete the second sentence, using the word given, so that it has a similar meaning to the first sentence. Do not change the word provided and use between three and six words in total. In the separate answer sheet, write your answers in capital letters, using one box per letter.

25 Rich knows everything about working with wood.

EXTENSIVE

Rich has an _____ of wood.

26 There is a possibility you might see something interesting, so take your camera.

HAPPEN

Take your camera _____ come across something interesting.

27 You must not, under any circumstances, submit your assignment late.

ACCOUNT

On _____ hand in your assignment late.

28 I really don't believe anything he said.

GRAIN

I doubt there _____ in what he said.

29 Mick decided not to go to the disco after all.

CHANGE

Mick had a _____ to the disco.

30 'Do you think you could help me move house next week?'

MIND

Would _____ move house next week.

Part 3: Word formation   8 marks

Write your answers in capital letters, using one box per letter.

17										
18										
19										
20									
21									
22									
23									
24								

Part 4: Key word transformation   12 marks

Write your answers in capital letters, using one box per letter.

(Answer boxes for questions 25–30)

Part 3: Word formation

8 marks

Write your answers in capital letters, using one box per letter.

17.
18.
19.
20.
21.
22.
23.
24.

Part 4: Key word transformation

12 marks

Write your answers in capital letters, using one box per letter.

25.

26.

27.

28.

29.

30.

Cambridge C1 Advanced Use of English

Test 10

Cambridge C1 Advanced Use of English

Part 1 — Multiple choice — **Test 10**

For questions 1–8, read the text below and decide which answer best fits each gap. In the separate answer sheet, mark the appropriate answer (A, B, C or D).

David Attenborough

If you are an **(1)**_____ viewer of nature documentaries you will no doubt be familiar with Sir David Attenborough, one of the most well-known and **(2)**_____ respected broadcasters and naturalists of all time.

(3)_____ the old saying, 'Never work with animals or children', Attenborough, who was born in 1926, in Isleworth, has spent most of his life exploring the world and its creatures from both sides of the lens. In 1952, in the TV series *Zoo Quest*, he received what could be **(4)**_____ as his initiation into combining television presenting with animals.

(5)_____, his career in television spanned many high-profile positions, including BBC2 Controller and Director of Programmes. In 1973 he resigned from his office-based role to **(6)**_____ on presenting and producing nature programmes for various British television networks.

Over the years, a special combination of incredible cinematography and Sir David's **(7)**_____ voice has produced prize-winning documentaries and brought the miracles of the planet Earth into millions of living rooms across the world.

His narrative style is strong and **(8)**_____, yet humble and soothing, and, whether he is describing the sound of insects at sunset in the Sahara, or describing a battle between predator and prey, his intonation lures you happily into the adventure.

1	A	avid	B	extreme	C	eager	D	interested
2	A	fully	B	highly	C	very	D	extremely
3	A	Despite	B	Although	C	In spite	D	Contrary
4	A	understood	B	said	C	described	D	known
5	A	Surely	B	Indeed	C	Clearly	D	Finally
6	A	rely	B	focus	C	determine	D	achieve
7	A	unmissable	B	unmistakable	C	unnoticeable	D	unclear
8	A	knowledgeable	B	knowable	C	alert	D	brainy

Cambridge C1 Advanced Use of English

Part 2 — Open cloze — Test 10

For questions 9–16, read the text below and decide which word best fits each gap. Use only one word for each gap. In the separate answer sheet, write your answers in capital letters, using one box per letter.

Watching paint dry

'Watching paint dry' is a term used to describe the witnessing of an incredibly boring event or situation. Typically, paint **(9)**_____ hours to dry, **(10)**_____ which time absolutely nothing appears to be happening. When painting the walls of a room, the paint should have dried enough for a second coat to be applied by the time all the walls have received one coat of paint.

Actually, depending on the type of paint used, the length of the drying process varies considerably. Oil-based paint, **(11)**_____ consists of pigment particles suspended in a drying agent, **(12)**_____ as linseed oil, is slow-drying and can be manipulated **(13)**_____ brush many hours after it first touches the canvas or wall. Water-based paint, **(14)**_____ the other hand, dries quickly, as do synthetic paints, which are most commonly used for painting interior walls.

Paint is stored as a liquid and dries as a solid, and the conversion process **(15)**_____ these two physical states involves the chemical combination of a resinous binding agent and a diluent, like water. It is clear **(16)**_____ the expression is used to describe observing a very boring and uneventful process.

Cambridge C1 Advanced Use of English
Part 3 — Word formation — Test 10

For questions 17–24, use the stem word on the right to form the correct word that fills each gap. In the separate answer sheet, write your answers in capital letters, using one box per letter.

Minecraft

Minecraft, the second-bestselling computer game of all time, was **(17)**_____ created in Sweden by a software developer named Markus Persson. — **ORIGIN**

The *Minecraft* game allows players to create their own three-dimensional environments out of a **(18)**_____ array of virtual building materials including stone, wood, glass or the useful power-source known as 'redstone'. — **MASS**

The endless **(19)**_____ of *Minecraft*, from building simple houses to recreations of entire cities or the bridge of the *Starship Enterprise*, have ensured its — **POSSIBLE**

(20)_____. — **POPULAR**

There are a number of *Minecraft* modes: 'Survival mode' requires the player to build defences against a range of enemies, including the shy but fearsome 'Enderman', while 'Creative mode' has **(21)**_____ resources to build. — **LIMIT**

In 2014, the software giant Microsoft bought the game for 2.5 billion dollars. One result of this has been the **(22)**_____ edition of *Minecraft*, which — **EDUCATE**
(23)_____ teachers to share their own creative ideas. School children can now use the game to learn about art or geometry, or to get — **COURAGE**
(24)_____ for creative writing assignments. — **INSPIRE**

Cambridge C1 Advanced Use of English

Part 4   Key word transformation   **Test 10**

For questions 25–30, complete the second sentence, using the word given, so that it has a similar meaning to the first sentence. Do not change the word provided and use between three and six words in total. In the separate answer sheet, write your answers in capital letters, using one box per letter.

25 She is very likely to get the job.
EVERY
She stands _____ the job.

26 Jan is the only person who knows about the plans for the party.
APART
No-one _____ of the plans for the party.

27 Most people think Graham has the ability to do whatever he wants in life.
CAPABLE
It is generally believed that Graham _____ whatever he wants in life.

28 He gave an explanation for making the mistake.
WHY
He explained the _____ the mistake.

29 I did not think about asking what you thought.
OCCURRED
It never _____ your opinion.

30 I do not intend to apologise, because it wasn't my fault.
INTENTION
I have _____ as it wasn't my fault.

Part 3: Word formation

8 marks

Write your answers in capital letters, using one box per letter.

17.
18.
19.
20.
21.
22.
23.
24.

Part 4: Key word transformation

12 marks

Write your answers in capital letters, using one box per letter.

25.
26.
27.
28.
29.
30.

Part 3: Word formation 8 marks

Write your answers in capital letters, using one box per letter.

17.
18.
19.
20.
21.
22.
23.
24.

Part 4: Key word transformation 12 marks

Write your answers in capital letters, using one box per letter.

25.
26.
27.
28.
29.
30.

Answers

Answers   Cambridge C1 Advanced Use of English   Test 1

Part 1: Multiple choice

1	B	amongst	5	B	despite
2	A	utilise	6	A	founding
3	C	lay	7	A	vindicate
4	D	confined	8	B	Whilst

Part 2: Open cloze

9	from	13	were
10	course	14	their
11	due / owing	15	as
12	of	16	such

Part 3: Word formation

17	harmful	21	invaluable
18	underground	22	teeth
19	cubic	23	absolutely
20	Amazingly	24	describing

Part 4: Key word transformation

25	would rather	not be
26	had no choice	but to
27	would have to / would need to / should / would	be put off
28	had he	started to sing / started singing
29	resulted in / had resulted in	him feeling
30	any objection to / an objection to	her coming to

© 2018 Prosperity Education – Use of English, Cambridge C1 Advanced and CAE are brands belonging to The Chancellor, Masters and Scholars of the University of Cambridge and are not associated with Prosperity Education or its apps, CAE Academy and FCE Academy

Answers   Cambridge C1 Advanced Use of English   Test 2

Part 1: Multiple choice					
1	A	known	5	C	period
2	C	instead	6	A	selling
3	B	manuscript	7	B	astute
4	B	come up with	8	D	entertainment

Part 2: Open cloze			
9	as	13	hence
10	only	14	of
11	Not	15	on / upon
12	which	16	in

Part 3: Word formation			
17	settlements	21	raiders
18	enduring	22	successfully
19	earliest	23	exploration
20	communities	24	newly

Part 4: Key word transformation		
25	point of view / view / point	strongly enough
26	it was high time	he left / to leave
27	only was the app / only was it	better in
28	makes it	worth working / worth working hard
29	aside from / except for / apart from	having a / a
30	being in	the public eye

© 2018 Prosperity Education – Use of English, Cambridge C1 Advanced and CAE are brands belonging to The Chancellor, Masters and Scholars of the University of Cambridge and are not associated with Prosperity Education or its apps, CAE Academy and FCE Academy

Answers   Cambridge C1 Advanced Use of English   Test 3

Part 1: Multiple choice

1	A	tradition	5	B	known as
2	C	undergoing	6	B	times
3	A	praises	7	B	myth
4	C	come in	8	C	present

Part 2: Open cloze

9	in	13	there
10	when / as	14	out
11	their	15	for
12	with / amongst	16	to

Part 3: Word formation

17	Championship	21	unpredictability
18	prestigious	22	retractable
19	ending	23	spectators
20	additionally	24	expensive

Part 4: Key word transformation

25	makes no / does not make a	difference to
26	he had	in mind
27	held in such	high
28	had always	come easily / come naturally
29	to have	been misinformed
30	the unlikely event	of you

© 2018 Prosperity Education – Use of English, Cambridge C1 Advanced and CAE are brands belonging to The Chancellor, Masters and Scholars of the University of Cambridge and are not associated with Prosperity Education or its apps, CAE Academy and FCE Academy

Answers Cambridge C1 Advanced Use of English Test 4

Part 1: Multiple choice

1	C	truly	5	C	users
2	B	emergence	6	A	owe
3	A	start-ups	7	B	imagine
4	D	completely	8	D	coining

Part 2: Open cloze

9	as	13	that
10	were	14	first / initially
11	by	15	since
12	into	16	are

Part 3: Word formation

17	fantastic	21	carefully
18	invention	22	importantly
19	majority	23	Publishing
20	perfecting	24	telling

Part 4: Key word transformation

25	was of	no consequence / little consequence
26	gradual rise	of / in / in its / in the
27	be a thorough	reappraisal of
28	he had arrived / he had been	on time
29	it illegal	to smoke
30	not to let	their children

© 2018 Prosperity Education – Use of English, Cambridge C1 Advanced and CAE are brands belonging to The Chancellor, Masters and Scholars of the University of Cambridge and are not associated with Prosperity Education or its apps, CAE Academy and FCE Academy

Answers   Cambridge C1 Advanced Use of English   Test 5

Part 1: Multiple choice

1	C	world-famous	5	D	outstanding
2	A	best-selling	6	B	pursue
3	B	layperson	7	A	suffered
4	B	gaining	8	C	confined

Part 2: Open cloze

9	after	13	big
10	of	14	where
11	between	15	never
12	by	16	to

Part 3: Word formation

17	doubtlessly / undoubtedly	21	infamous
18	remarkable	22	recount
19	fishermen	23	definitely
20	magnificent	24	additions

Part 4: Key word transformation

25	was unaware	of his problems / of problems
26	in the mood	for going to / to go to / for
27	failed to recognise / failed to acknowledge	the importance
28	any improvement	in your health / to your health / in her health / to her health
29	as soon as	we receive / we have received
30	had not	put up

Answers   Cambridge C1 Advanced Use of English   Test 6

Part 1: Multiple choice						
1	A	set up	5	A	phenomenal
2	C	initially	6	C	requests
3	B	however	7	A	stiff
4	D	general	8	C	points out

Part 2: Open cloze			
9	from	13	than
10	during / for / at / throughout	14	which
11	in	15	part
12	with / attracting / achieving	16	in

Part 3: Word formation			
17	impressive	21	thought
18	significance	22	sunk
19	hugely	23	explanation
20	naval	24	historians

Part 4: Key word transformation		
25	interruption was	caused by
26	it had not	been for
27	with the exception	of Peter came
28	was due to	take off / have taken off
29	sorry that / sorry	he could not
30	no matter	how hard

© 2018 Prosperity Education – Use of English, Cambridge C1 Advanced and CAE are brands belonging to The Chancellor, Masters and Scholars of the University of Cambridge and are not associated with Prosperity Education or its apps, CAE Academy and FCE Academy

Answers   Cambridge C1 Advanced Use of English   Test 7

Part 1: Multiple choice

1	A	industry	5	A	output
2	B	referred	6	C	forefront
3	D	brought	7	A	changes
4	B	innovation	8	B	strived

Part 2: Open cloze

9	which / that	13	by / amongst
10	the	14	despite
11	in / by / through	15	to
12	known	16	most / and

Part 3: Word formation

17	famous	21	hexagonal
18	Northern	22	disappear
19	greatest	23	neighbouring
20	volcanic	24	Scottish

Part 4: Key word transformation

25	came across	as being / as
26	made no	reference to
27	is nothing / has nothing	to do with
28	has risen / has sharply	sharply / risen
29	at the point	of leaving
30	not so	problematic / problem prone

© 2018 Prosperity Education – Use of English, Cambridge C1 Advanced and CAE are brands belonging to The Chancellor, Masters and Scholars of the University of Cambridge and are not associated with Prosperity Education or its apps, CAE Academy and FCE Academy

Answers — Cambridge C1 Advanced Use of English — Test 8

Part 1: Multiple choice

1	B	according	5	A	memorable
2	C	Whether	6	A	portrayed
3	A	accounts	7	A	traced
4	D	associated	8	C	adapted

Part 2: Open cloze

9	such	13	by
10	either / whether	14	in
11	to	15	able
12	their	16	the

Part 3: Word formation

17	commercial	21	maximising
18	deregulation	22	comparatively / comparably
19	businessman / businessperson	23	competitor / competitive
20	Currently	24	dominance

Part 4: Key word transformation

25	resulted in	the cancellation
26	far as music	is concerned
27	high time	you got / you found
28	in with	a chance of
29	made a great / made an	impression
30	preparation may / preparation could / preparation might	cost us

© 2018 Prosperity Education – Use of English, Cambridge C1 Advanced and CAE are brands belonging to The Chancellor, Masters and Scholars of the University of Cambridge and are not associated with Prosperity Education or its apps, CAE Academy and FCE Academy

Answers — Cambridge C1 Advanced Use of English — Test 9

Part 1: Multiple choice

1	A	flagship	5	A	wonderful
2	B	widely watched	6	B	close-to-the-bone
3	A	estimated	7	A	focuses
4	C	essence	8	A	guaranteed

Part 2: Open cloze

9	with	13	into
10	speaking	14	joined
11	full	15	own
12	developed / got	16	after

Part 3: Word formation

17	youngster	21	incredibly
18	attention	22	failure
19	Championships / Championship	23	generation
20	achievement	24	respective

Part 4: Key word transformation

25	extensive working / extensive	knowledge / understanding
26	in case you	happen to
27	no account	should you / can you / must you
28	is a / was a	grain of truth
29	change of	mind about going / heart about going
30	you mind	helping me to / helping me

© 2018 Prosperity Education – Use of English, Cambridge C1 Advanced and CAE are brands belonging to The Chancellor, Masters and Scholars of the University of Cambridge and are not associated with Prosperity Education or its apps, CAE Academy and FCE Academy

Answers — Cambridge C1 Advanced Use of English — Test 10

Part 1: Multiple choice

1	A	avid	5	B	Indeed	
2	B	highly	6	B	focus	
3	A	Despite	7	B	unmistakable	
4	C	described	8	A	knowledgeable	

Part 2: Open cloze

9	takes	13	by
10	during / in	14	on
11	which	15	between
12	such	16	why / that

Part 3: Word formation

17	originally	21	unlimited / limitless
18	massive	22	educational
19	possibilities	23	encourages
20	popularity	24	inspiration

Part 4: Key word transformation

25	every	chance of getting / likelihood of getting
26	apart from	Jan knows
27	is capable / is more than capable	of doing
28	reason	why he made
29	occurred to me	to ask / to ask you
30	no intention of	apologising

© 2018 Prosperity Education – Use of English, Cambridge C1 Advanced and CAE are brands belonging to The Chancellor, Masters and Scholars of the University of Cambridge and are not associated with Prosperity Education or its apps, CAE Academy and FCE Academy

Notes

Notes

Printed by Amazon Italia Logistica S.r.l.
Torrazza Piemonte (TO), Italy